Thoughts Of A Fool

*star-crossed with empathy

Natalie Serse

/ BookLeaf
Publishing

India | USA | UK

Made with ❤ on the BookLeaf Publishing Platform
www.bookleafpub.in
www.bookleafpub.com

Dedication

This is dedicated to the "people that lived above the buildings that I was hustling in front of, called the police on me when I was just trying to make some money to feed my daughter..."

Kidding. I dedicate this honest work to myself and all whom I love dearly.

-Biggie

Preface

My superpower is also my curse. It elevates me and depletes me all the same. These are just some thoughts. I hope you enjoy a tour of my mind.

Acknowledgements

My Family.

1. many moons

I'm here. I'm sitting on the grassy bank of the Mississippi River surrounded by dragonflies playing a beautifully choreographed game of tag. The setting sun shines so brightly and sweetly kisses all below. It makes the water ripples glisten, icy silver blue dancing their own dance onto the shore. The grass, freshly cut, is green and brown. Alive and dead. But somehow, crisp all the same. The dragonflies sweep in and out, glowing like magic fairies. When the sun's rays catch a translucent wing, they twinkle. The colors could not be more vibrant. The sun could not feel more protective, comforting and loving, telling us that it's going to be ok. And it's all so very beautiful. The dragonflies swarm, black and blue wings flutter rapidly and on beat. They swarm around my head, going to where they're going, then coming right back. They move faster than the dragonflies I met a bit further south on the New Orleans banks of the River. Those dragonflies are more poised, more friendly. They used to come and sit on my arms. Unload for a bit. But these dragonflies are different. They're lively and youthful and magnificently playful. And they swarm around me glistening in the grass. It feels so familiar like I've been here before. And they welcome me back. Because I've been here before, many moons ago. Many Moons Ago on the Mighty Mississippi. And it brings such joyous tears to my eyes. And I think how fucking lucky am I?

2. Little Bird Hoyt

Little Bird, I hear you
Blowing kisses across the forest to me
Such a beautiful melody,
Soundtrack to my heart
The trees twinkle, water stars sparkle on hanging moss
They flash oh so gently to the rhythm of our kisses
Birds chirp in the distance singing our chorus
Crunch of the stone and brush under our feet keeps time,
The beat of our hearts.
And you begin blowing kisses again
Steadily like a metronome keeping count for all of the
forest
And I kiss along, in unison
We are so much more beautiful when we are intertwined
as one.

With each gentle breeze, the branches sway,
Dancing like lovers, caught in a play.
Whispering secrets, the leaves spin and twirl,
As twilight descends, our magic unfurls.
The sky blushes softly, a canvas of gold,
Painting our stories, forever retold.
In this moment, we rise beyond time,
Little Bird, together, in perfect rhyme.

3. Alive

What do I feel inside? It's a fullness to be alive. Like you ate too much food at Thanksgiving, and now your skinny jeans are a little bit too hard to fit in. It swells in your chest, not your stomach, your heart. A circadian rhythm in time with the earth's. As we spin into new movements, the pulse quickens or slows. The sporadic changes in tempo ignite this ebb and flow. In and out, your heart is full and fluctuating. Exhilarating then placating. Syncopating then elongating. Sometimes way too fast to control, the energy takes over your soul, wrenching your heart in half, diverting to opposite poles. The agony heightens as the drumbeat accelerates. Louder and faster, it reverberates. And then, without warning, it comes to a halt. A reprieve for a moment, then sweeps into a graceful waltz. Romantic and elegant, calming and pacifying. You find yourself smiling, breathing, sighing. It's a ride with no seatbelt, no helmets or nets. It frightens, then shelters, then tosses; get ready to catch! It's a fullness to be alive, so vibrant, this mess. Ride in the moment without fear of what's next. Breathe in with your heart, exhale, acquiesce. Such beauty in the ritual, anxiety suppressed. Grateful and humbled. You are favored and blessed.

4. Circus

She stands out, stands up in the spotlight
Thousands come to watch her perform
She puts on her hat, looks up to the crowd
They clap and they cheer and some roar in excitement
She waves her hands up, open and ready
Now let the countdown begin.
Cue up the harps and the violins,
The strings and the winds.
Exhilaration as the energy spins.
She inhales, exhales the breath from within
Her hands drop and the pizzicato begins
The band starts to play at her whim
She moves right, they ascend, they crescendo
She moves left, they descend to the innuendo
That she is the show
But what they don't know
Is she's in full control.
With her hands raised, she accesses their souls.
The good with the bad, the innocent and the tarnished
The melody flows. What a beautiful sonnet!
Their insecurities strummed away by the guitarist.
She plays them meticulously with her power harnessed
She takes on their traumas like a poisonous harvest
Bountiful, beautiful, poisonous harvest

Filling her up to the point of unrest.
So she stops and she screams,
So cursed and so blessed.
This maniacal grace only she can posses.
It burns in her soul, pumps her heart through her chest
She now waives her hands, up down, east west
Screaming in rage, harmony to contest.
What a cursed gift to bequest!
She heals as she takes, controlling the pace.
Until she can't take no more...
Tears roll down her face,
Hair tousled and perfectly placed out of place.
Running breathless to the end of the race,
She gives them her all as she takes off their plates.
Nothing left to give, she dissipates into herself.
She can't complain, these were the cards she was dealt.
She grows stronger and stronger with each performance
Manipulating their sorrows to joy by transformance.
She serves as she takes, energy depletes.
She can't breathe anymore.
She falls from her feet.
Crawling to safety, yearning to retreat.
Let go. Please let go.
It's time to release.

5. Die

they say a Phoenix lives 972 times longer than we do.
but they die

Rise from the ashes,
Isn't that the mantra?

Be it a bird
Be it a flower
Be it a weed
Be it some lava

It's the bounce back game
When nothing is left
Down and out, dying
Then come back renewed, reborn, refreshed
Better than the rest.
Better than the best.

It could be the ultimate "Fuck You"
Rather, it's done with grace
After all, you've burned up in flames
Then dramatically recreated from the remains
Regenerated by fate, a new life awaits

Different city, different state
It's all yours to take
But.

You do it with grace.

So, burn bright, my baby
Scorching fiery flashes
Allow yourself to surrender your life,
Surrender to the circumstances.
Die so horribly, rise so artistically

What an extraordinary life this is,
The true story of what romance is.
Such a powerfully beautiful concept this conquest is
When life can be reclaimed from the ashes

6. edicius

I can understand why people commit suicide. The thought of cutting open a vein, allowing the blood to pour out seems satisfying, therapeutic, healing almost, as if the warm, blue liquid needs to be changed out every so often like an oil change on a car. Maintenance. As if that blood is tainted, clouded by years of disappointment, failure, heartbreak and sadness. If we pour it out, let it flow, flush it out, clean it through, we can come out refreshed and renewed on the other end. In ancient times, doctors would bleed patients to heal them. It makes sense. It's almost as if the body calls for it. The difference, however, is that there rarely is a medical professional in the room with you these days to monitor. So, you cut. You bleed. Fast and uncontrollable, without a new supply being pumped back in, without the fresh blood, fresh life being replenished. You just bleed out the old until you run cold. No more warmth circulating within. No more sadness or pain to endure. It sounds beautifully sweet, romantic even. If only we could empty out what's inside then we could start over new. Clean Slate. But even more sadly, it just doesn't work that way.

7. Memphis

You drove me to madness

Machiavellian and masterfully,
You drove me to madness.
Taught me so much, showed
Me the way up the Mighty,
Guided by dragonflies and metaphors.
Messages magnified by
Madness & Metaphors.
Magically meaningful messages
Magnified by Madness & Metaphors.
What a fucking mindfuck.

8. Mermaid

There once was a lady who lived in the sea.
She could swim like a fish and grew feet at the beach.
She was more than quite lovely, generous and kind
Her aura, a deep pink and purple design
She was a Goddess, Love in life form
Radiating empathy and ruby adorned

Multiple times before this,
She crossed paths with a Starfish
Who more than just caught her eye.
He was gilded and regal, humble, ethereal.
He might just be her perfect guy.

These short interactions left her heart asking
'Who are you, I want to know more?'
He received her message under the water
And asked her to meet by the shore.

They talked and they laughed, and they enjoyed their
day
Until the tide crashed in and pulled him away
A wave from the east rolled in like a beast
Placing him far out to sea.
Too far to reach, too far to see

She knew that's where he's meant to be.
He grew larger and larger the further he drifted.
And his light was ignited out in the distance so vivid.
Shining so brightly, controlling with magic
Noble and Knightly, enigmatic, dynamic
He was a High Priest, so beautifully dramatic.

Her work in this place was not yet complete
So she stayed behind to serve and heal those in need
And on each new moon, he would retreat from the sea
To visit his Goddess and find ease in her peace
With love and respect, she was his release
And he was her King and High Priest

One thing's for certain.
Their love is timeless.
In water or land,
They'll float hand in hand.
Or in the sky shining like diamonds.

9. Vagabond

I love you all.
But I must let go and keep going.
For those of you who stay, thank you.
For those of you who float away, I'll always remember
the good times.
I love you all.
But I will keep going. Growing.
The limits are none. Non-existent.
And thus, sadness fills my heart, swells in my throat.
You're all living your own life anyhow.
So, I let go. I can't hold onto something that is not mine.
I have to create love everywhere
And I want to see what the world has to offer
I want to meet the people, taste the food, drink the
drinks and dance the dances
And to do that, I have to let go.
I will love you all the same, perhaps even more
Absence. Heart. Fonder.
You've heard that before. Now, living it, I see it's truth.
When the time has come, I have to go.
And I will carry all of you with me in my heart.
You give me the strength to continue on my journey.
And with that, we are always together.

And I am never alone.

So as I tread this winding road,
With corners sharp and paths unknown,
I'll cherish every moment shared,
Each laughter, every kindness shown.
Through every challenge I embrace,
Your love will guide, a steadfast flame,
In the tapestry of lives entwined,
Though distance grows, my heart remains.
An echo of the lives we've lived,
A melody that lingers sweet,
In every sunset's soft goodbye,
I'll find you there, where soulmates meet.

10. Some random thoughts

It's time, and I'm here. Just me, this coffee, and this group of kids debating whether they should do something or go home and be weird. Midway through their convo, they change topics. Now they are discussing which facial features they get from their respective parents. It's decided. Monica gets her nose from her father but her eye shape from her mother. They all laugh and decide to go to Washington Square Park instead of being weird and going home. They are gone. Now it's just me and my coffee.

All that was needed was just a splash of lavender.
That's all.

It felt unreal, exhilarating. I was alive.
Like riding, doing 60, around Lake Pontchratrain, no
helmet, wind caressing your face, fancy fuckin free.
That's living to me.

Most people want materialistic wealth, tangible and shiny things. Some may have sold their soul for a price, ducats in the account. More money, less soul. Never enough, always needing more. That's not it for me. Give me connections. I want to explore, converse, wander,

touch and feel energies. Vibrate with and against
frequencies. I want to grow my soul while leaving a
positive impression, part of my aura, behind. I have a
home deep inside that I am able to take with me
anywhere. It welcomes adventure and heart
fulfillment. It cherishes beauty in simplicity. I want to be
soul-rich. That kind of wealth never runs out. It only
grows.

As I fly over NYC on this hazy day, I spot buildings I
helped erect, adding dimension to the iconic
skyline. How amazing is that? I will forever be a part of
this city. I will forever be New York.

As he walked past,
I could smell him so strongly.
And so sure that he could smell me.
He smelled of amber, vanilla, tobacco, patchouli
And I smelled of pretty green trees.

I love when an insect accepts the invitation to land on
your hand.

A sweetly satisfying sensation encompasses my soul. I
close my eyes and see you. And I smile.

The world speaks to you. All you have to do is listen.

11. Lover's Eyes

Give me a love that stops time.
A reason to slow down, to stop running.
Bring alive my dreams from night to sunlight
Let go of fear
Let go of inhibitions
Love without restriction
Dance it for the world to see
Scream it with conviction
Make my heart stop when you look in my eyes
Bring life to a halt and completely unwind
Life frozen in time when our two souls combine
Passionately yours.
Forever mine.
You fit perfectly within and without the lines
A classic concerto played in perfect time
"A lover's eyes will gaze an eagle blind"
Shakespearean sonnet recitations in mind
Burning auras intertwined
Hot like fire. And fine like wine.
Please, oh please.
Give me your all.
Give me your love.
A love that stops time.

12. Dear You

Thank you for holding me in a time where anxiety snapped off synapses in my head like popcorn popping in a pan. You held me when I did not know anything, not even myself. Thank you for holding me when I was a huge pain in your ass. Thank you for holding me when my emotions engulfed me - and all reasoning. Thank you for holding me and showing me what being loved feels like. Thank you for setting that bar. And if I could come across something remotely close, then that would be a blessing.

13. Blue Dream

Do you dream?
Because I do.
I dream of possibilities.
Beautifully curated and meticulously detailed
possibilities.
Endless possibilities.
Some out of my control, some attainable.
Colorful and wistful "what if's" weave through my brain
in never ending ways.
Most times I can't finish a thought, as another possibility
crosses the path
And another turn is taken.

Is it bad to prefer the dream world?
I love it so much that I escape any chance I get.
Lucid dreaming allows me to pick up where I left off the
night before.
And I am enamored with it.

But what am I supposed to do with these dreams?
Do I share them?
Are they my therapy, private secrets to keep to myself?
Am I addicted to them?
Is it harmful to retreat into myself?

Am I missing out on real life possibilities?

Dear Dreams, My Dear Dreams,
My Solace, My Retreat.
Oh, Dreams.
What is this hold you have on me?
So sad, as it seems,
You must be released.
My Dreams,
So Bittersweet,
So Incomplete.
What do you do to me?
Dear Dreams. My Dear Dreams.
My Reality.
My Solace. My Retreat.

14. Bubbles

Orbiting, swirling in circles, feathering through force
fields otherwise repulsive
Now allowing you in, slowly but surely
Energies merge when otherwise on different planes
Picking up particles otherwise propelled away
They are yours now for the taking
Redirection created by conscious direction
Navigation system powered by the mind's eye
This is where you bloom like the moon
This is where you thrive as is your right
This is where you belong all along
For now anyhow

15. Skin

Skin so uncomfortable
Scratchy itchy
Too loose and too tight
Too cold and too warm
Slippery slimey

Need to get out
Need to breathe
Need some water
Need some sleep
Need to run
Need to rage
Need to break free from this cage

I'm suffocating and can't get enough air
Reaching out for help
But no one is there
The sun feels too hot and the rain feels too cold
Everything is wrong and it hurts
I can't find a safe place, No friendly faces
Tried it all. There's nothing that works
I want to run and I want to stay
My insides are at war with themselves
Don't know who I am. Don't know what I want.

But I need a purge. I need to cleanse
I need to find me again
I'm shedding my skin
It's not mine anymore
I'm dying right now
Not really alive right now
I don't know anything anymore

Kundalini has intervented
Welcome to your conception
All you've ever known is gone
So you surrender to acception
Skin so uncomfortable
Scratchy and itchy
Regenerating as it should
Into something different, into something new
It has been accepted
It has been understood
The stars in the sky tell the truth.

You are forming into you.

16. so love.

It's on fire.

Golden embers, pink and orange, light the sky.

Burning gently but so bright hot.

Then there's this fade to purple where the fire cools.

It's the perfect color combination, marrying the day and night where they ignite.

It's the most beautiful vision.

Everyone should be able to see this.

How it subtly reflects into the marina, glistening across the glassy blue, softly vibrating waves paying tribute to the beautiful union above.

And lucky for me to be an invited guest to this wedding of light and dark, of night and day, the prophesized fusion with passion so full it burns visibly across the horizon. So perfect. So grateful.

So love.

17. Dance

Pink room, filled with toys
Posters, dolls, and sadness.
Canopy bed lined with stuffed animals
Perfectly placed to protect her from the madness.
She spent hours in there, lost in her dreams
To be known. To be heard. To be accepted.
To dance her way wildly out of the box they created.

It's ok to think. It's ok to laugh.
It's ok to sing with the flowers at a sunbath.
It's ok to be different. Be ok to be free
Little girl, laugh, scream, smile.
Be happy.
Let down your guard. Put down your fists.
Unclench your teeth and release your grip.
One day you'll be free to be free
So retreat to your space, confined and safe
Safe to dance, dance, the tension away

18. Just some advice

It's the ultimate goal for many. A right of passage,
necessity. A must.
It's what little girls dream of, families plan for. A ritual of
tradition and fluff.
A beautiful wedding, flowers and lace.
Velvet and satin and paint on your face.
This is the best day of your life.
You are becoming a wife!
They adorn you in gilded kitchen appliances and linens
all white
Now you have a place in the world.
Look how far you've come, precious! Make your skirt
twirl!
Overdone flowers detailed with sequins and pearls.
Each movement and smile so perfectly rehearsed.
What a beautiful sentence. To have and to hold.
It's all you could ask for, all you could hope.

Perhaps I am jaded.
The judgement rings loud.
But so romantic! They wrote their own vows!
Husband and Wife! you are pronounced.
And tonight you will find out just how endowed....
But right now, dear precious, in front of the crowd

With rings of gold meant only to bound
You, dear precious, to your espoused
Dancing above in the heavenly clouds.
Your King, His Queen. Pass down the crown.
The landscape has been painted.
Fairytale renowned.
Remember now, precious, this is paramount!
Remain his possession.
Devoted, devout.
But keep your flame bright, true to yourself
And don't let any mother fucker ever blow that shit out.

19. Love Stuff

Lead with love
Live with love
Love with love, pouring out
Wild rapids from your heart
Love overflowing, drowning everything else
Unstoppable current whisking you away
Don't try to swim against it. It will pull you back.
And when you stop trying to fight it,
You realize how peaceful the ride is when you just let go.
Lead with love
Live with love
Love with love

I want you
Your playful drizzle
Your visionary hail
Your sexy rain
Your beautiful snow
Your focused ice
Your loving haze
Your brilliant vapor
Your resilient steam
Your protective sleet

Your positive powder
Your intoxicating monsoon
I want your loyal waterfall
I want you
I want it all
I am ready

I want that deep, can't live without you love.
That take over your solar plexus love
That lightning shooting from your heart love
That glittery eyes, dilated pupil love
That stay ready to fuck, anytime, anyplace love
That embrace feels like home love
That found my best friend love
That think of you every minute love
That consuming, giving you air to breathe love
That want to scream it from the top of the highest
building love
That trust you with my life love
That your face makes me smile love
That do anything for you love
That make me feel like a kid again love

20. Hmmm

Do you believe we exist in alternate universes, realities, existences? That there are different versions of you? You ever get the feeling you know someone or placed yourself somewhere before? What is deja vu? Are our alternate lives running simultaneously? Or are these past lives we are viewing, centuries in the making? When this version of you dies, is there another, on a different frequency that dies too? When you die, do all the truths speak true? Do you get the answers to those deja vus? Do you remember that person you met that you thought you knew? Only to learn that you did, and they knew you too! And what about some things you maybe saw yourself do? Then you learn the alternate you does all kinds of different shit too. When a version of you dies, are your dreams answered too? Are those creepy recurring ones warnings to you from Frequency You.2? Sending messages or clues as to what you should do? Or are those glitchy moments in the matrix where the messages can sneak through? I believe in these alternate lives in alternate universes. I really do.

21. Socio

She sits on the edge of the river as dragonflies dance in
her hair
People unload all their problems, and she poses as if she
cares.
See, she was given a gift at birth, a gift that she views as
a curse.
She can heal people with empathy, and all of their
nonsense becomes hers.
Most empaths are grateful for the chance to help others.
She'd rather rip her eyes out than listen to these
motherfuckers.
They talk. She does not listen.
Instead, she smiles. So enchanting.
She absorbs their troubles 'til they see good in
themselves
Such a noble gift to possess, one that her existence
repels.
To hear about their problems, she really could care less.
She's thinking about many other things, I hate to
confess.
Her emotional intelligence is way greater than theirs.
She plays with them, manipulating despair.
The dragonflies dance; she really is charming.
So beautiful and gentle, she's uninterested, my darling.

She's cold to the bone, internally distant.
She's mean to her own mother. She's narcissistic.
She cares only for herself and a very select few.
Her curse forces her to pretend she cares for you too.
Selfish and proud, she's her number one fan.
She might like a few of them, but most she can't stand.
She'd rather be home, safe all alone.
Or doing whatever she wants.
She really is an asshole
But she loves you with all of her heart.

www.ingramcontent.com/pod-product-compliance
Lightning Source LLC
Chambersburg PA
CBHW050959030426
42339CB00007B/399